Crownfeathers and Effigies

Crownfeathers and Effigies

Jerry Bradley

LAMAR UNIVERSITY Press

Beaumont, Texas

Library of Congress Cataloging-in-Publication Data

Bradley, Jerry, 1948 –
   Crownfeathers and Effigies / Jerry Bradley

   ISBN 978-0-9850838-3-0

   2014
   2014932378

Design by Minor Design

Acknowledgments

The author gratefully acknowledges the following publications
in which versions of these poems appeared:

Ahimsa: "The Problem of Angels"
CCTE Studies: "Pity Poor Mercalli"
Chest: "Chemo Ward at Texas Children's Hospital"
Chili Verde Review: "Unmade Love"
Cities: A Book of Poems: "Pictures from London"
The Connecticut Review: "Continental Drift"
Descant: "Finding Your Way in the Dark," "Sorry Seconds,"
    "Subject-Verb-Complement"
Explorers: A Collection of Contemporary Literature:
    "Bad Coffee Is Grounds for Divorce"
Halcyon: "Gator Eye"
Harvests of New Millennium: "Indelicate"
Houston Poetry Fest 2012 Anthology: "An Old Familiar Offering"
Illya's Honey: "Geography Lesson"
The Kerf: "Moonlight and Peaches," "Planetary Texas"
Modern Poetry Studies: "Estrangement"
New Texas: "If You're Drinking To Forget, Please Pay in Advance,"
    "Oscar Wilde Visits Walt Whitman"
Oklahoma Poems, and Their Poets: "Another Thing To Lament"
Old Crow Review: "Letter to B.," "Writer's Block"
The Plowman Anthology: A Poem to Daddy: "Reliable Sources"
Poetry and the City: "Pictures from London"
Porcupine Literary Arts Magazine: "The Missing"
Red River Review: "Belling the Vampire," "Bonaventure Cemetery, Savannah,"
    "Family Thrift," "Hollywood Metonymic," "Primer"
Right Hand Pointing: "A New Cosmology"
Rockhurst Review: "This Close"
San Pedro River Review: "Gull in the Canyon," "Out Here,"
    "The Texas Country Reporter Interviews the Famous Poet"
Slant: "Running with Scissors"
Taj Mahal Review: "Andrea del Sarto Lectures about Poetry," "At the Arcade,"
    "At the End," "Bad Day at the Psychic Fair," "Listen to the Trees"
Texas Poetry Calendar 2011: "I Remember"
32 Poems: "Monoxide"
Voices de la Luna: "No One Else To Say It"
Writing Texas: "Evil Twins," "Lonesome," "The Woman Who Disliked Kissing"

for all the grand ones

Cecilia, Lillian, Gus, Lucy, John, Caroline, and Robinson

thanks for making old J-Dog legitimate

Contents

broken glass

reel life and others

enlarged hearts

absorbed, inhaled, or ingested

broken glass

Primer

In third grade I fell in love with my teacher,
an indecency I know, but Miss Heusinger's eyes
opened and closed in our sunny classroom,
well, like a pupil. Aside from a single afternoon
of cleaning the chalk trays, she was a woman
whom I almost never stood near. She married,
moved away; it was her policy, I learned,
not to leave no child behind. A substitute finished the term.

That is how a heart learns to break ... then
life repeats itself. The trouble with redundancy
is there is just too much of it.

Years later she is likely divorced,
abandoned by a man who wasn't good enough,
or has died. But she is still one of them —
the ones we are doomed to remember —
and, call it what you will, never quite quit loving.
You may remember what your first love said
when you met, but you couldn't see the future,
how she held it like an eraser in her uplifted hand.

Pictures from London

Your e-mail arrives with a slide show of your trip
and dizzying Lucy Ricardo reports:
the Tim's River loosing its ships,
tourists outside Buckminster Cathedral,
but no photos of Pig Pen, the clock —
just you and a cabbie in front of Royal Alfred Hall.
They remind that you and I are no longer young,
these timed IED's that frame after frame
threaten our mother tongue.

The last — I hope — shows a barmaid from St. Pauli's.
You say you wish I were there; I wish
so too. Better to see with my own eyes
what you have failed to hear with yours.
We are not accustomed to other worlds,
but I thank you for the shots,
the XO hug-and-kiss, and, yes,
that surprise from Harold's you promise.

This Is Summer

What the water says,
    it says to the pines,
        and the rail lines

to the locomotive.
    Neither offers a good place
        to recline.

The sparrows skitter and scream
    above the bus stop with no orchestra
        to finish their act,

like the briary bleats of the saxman
    whose confession defies the recordings
        that caught him.

The church is beautiful,
    but only the poem says
        what cannot be said:

this flutter, these serviceable gods
    pay homage to crownfeathers
        and effigies,

the bill that swipes
    across a branch
        and calls itself summer.

An Old Familiar Offering

– for Shawn

Money isn't everything, but it sure keeps the kids in touch.
An e-mail from one reminds about a birthday soon.
Things are good, he says;
he's working part-time, but cash is tight,
and by the way he has just quit school.

Like God, he needs money, always has —
and like his mother spends it.
He prefers to disobey both and, still a teen,
talks out of both sides of his ass.

But I too have been known not to listen to good advice,
so I sign the check and lick the flap,
offer congratulations for another year gone.
In time another holiday will roll around;
I'll hear from him again before the seasons are done.

And what could a man with no standing write?
Get a GED? Stay clean? Have fun?
There's not much I can tell him for fact
he doesn't already know except that
Your class reunions won't likely be much fun.

Fishing for Snook at Sea

Moored near the pilings beneath a former highway bridge,
I pull out the Shimanos and bait — pinfish,
greenbacks, and finger mullet — and give her
her choice. "Cast into the shade," I remind,
"and use a light grip — like so."
I press her hand around mine.

We whip the rod and froth the air;
we need to keep the leaders short,
and I fix them to the braided line.
"They're made of lead, so why
don't we call them ledders?" she asks.
I pinch the flared barbs down tight.

I ask her to whisper and put
a finger to my lips. "Shhh!"
But she is tired of instructions.
"Can't we just fish?"

I tell her we'll be catching dinner soon,
but hours later without a bite she is in full pout.
She puts down her rod and asks,
"Couldn't we just get a case of crabs instead?"

"It's a box," I tease. "A box."
She snorts and takes her line out,
fiddles with the lure on her hat.
I say again, "Don't scare the fish."
"Scare them?" she says. "Wouldn't
pulling them in the boat do that?"

Geography Lesson

He began by erasing the oceans from the map.
He had no blue, so he filled the seas with land
and colored new countries, invented capitals
where factories hummed and the military paraded
in the cathedral square while the Committee to Safeguard Ourselves
watched on. He penciled in ghost towns
and unnamed metropolises whose exports filled the fields,
drew mountain ranges where goats grazed butterfly-laden hills.

There was yellow in the box, so he drew the sun;
he couldn't tell how things would go wrong.
Since there was no water, the moon no longer held sway.
It hung lost overhead like the lovers below
who bared their teeth in a warning smile
and wept when no serenades were sung.

Bonaventure Cemetery, Savannah

This place is punishment for our oldest sin:
the Wilmington frames the azaleas and statuary,
and avenues of oaks draped with long moss provide reprieve
from the ragged field and oystershell road.
So it's not a bad spot to end.

But since it is a place where journeys mostly cease,
we should accept its glad tidings as we go,
the cheery *bon voyage*, the good fortune its name commends.
It's not as though we're bound somewhere else or on vacation;
death may be a new undertaking, but it's not a new business
for which we should be wished "good luck in your new location."

It is, as we've always known, where the leather pays the toll;
it is where after the war Muir stalled on his thousand-mile walk
from Indiana to the Keys.
                                    Blind for a month,
he saw in the darkness how his life must change.
And what he saw, he saw again where the salt marsh
gave way to plantation and then these graves.

Waiting for money, he found himself
amid thickets of sparkleberry and for five nights
took his rest among the speechless dead
        where he first dreamed the West.

Crownfeathers and Effigies

Gull in the Canyon

Lost as Coronado, he circles
the caprock escarpment, then veers,
chevrons winging toward the hackberries.

Camped near the shelterbelt conifers,
we too are far away from home,
caught between the paleohunters

who first wandered here ages ago
and left their curved knives for museums
and the pilots from New Mexico

whose stealth fighters *kaboom* long after
they have hied out of sight. It's not just
the limestone that is impervious:

we too are unyielding, like sand,
the siltstone beneath our feet, boulder
fields that obscure the trail, cottonwoods

bearing their freight of hawks. It is hot,
and the thermals keep him soaring
high above our tent where the rainfly keeps

out only the dust. Those poor Spaniards!
When hail stampeded their horses and
broke their crockery, they didn't head

for home — certainly not at once.
They couldn't fly, neither could they see
Texas 256 just beyond

the gypsum domes (speed limit posted
but unenforced) or the overlook
where the jawbones of bison still lay.

But they could see stars — those last shiny
aquifers of silver that shone straight
on the Seven Cities like small change.

Their dreams on the darkest nights were
as vacant as this gull-less land
and as empty as their saddlebags of gold.

Lonesome

When George Gobel told the Rat Pack he felt
like a pair of brown shoes, we understood.
"Well then there now," he said
as if anticipating the failed surgery ahead.

Hank Sr. knew the moan of whippoorwills and trains
and nearly wept, and Dylan's maid
bore a large family yet died a friendless death,
done in by a casually-tossed cane.

Patchen said our lives were meaningless
because the years were cruel;
then he fell off an OR table,
another paralyzed fool

until he too found his remedy among the dead.
And it echoes among us at every turn:
on the trail of the pine, in Bill Monroe's Kentuckiana sound
and McCarthy's apocalyptic border town,

when Elvis wonders if we are tonight.
In time even the unhurried tortoise
reaches the end of the line.
Slowed by the entropy of words, we know

that what we say is seldom what we mean
(even when uttered to the slenderest soul).
Call it our unpaid debt to the Phoenecians
for letters and the Maya (of course)
who in their misery first understood the need for 0.

Last Ride Down

On May 31, 2003, the Devil's Highway, U.S. Route 666, was changed to 491.

The Devil, they say, is in the design,
but there is little room for him in Utah.
A road with few options,
not even twenty miles' worth,
it flees Mormon Monticello
and Abajo Peak's frowning brow
before declining toward Dove Creek.

In Colorado it's just horse farms
and the first aroma of fry bread
Can we stop at Cutthroat Castle?
The auto graveyard opposite the Church of Christ
offers the first clue; then it's southeast
to the Cortez Drive-In's twin screens
that stare at one another like forbidding parents
until suddenly it's Broadway.

The Anasazi Lounge still offers free refills,
but it sits at 664 now
though the building's never moved,
three 6's too inviting for skinwalkers
and shapeshifters who fear the fiend in their heart
more than one on the highway or the next stool.

We admire the wisdom of the Indians;
they are not afraid of God –
but they are afraid of religion.
According to the Gospel Lighhouse,
it is the Christian curse on the Navajo,
its marquee wondering, *If you don't
feel close to God, guess who moved?*

But savages can misunderstand
the Bible as easily as a map.

They distrust men with marked foreheads
and inked arms. They do, however, trust gambling,
and at the Ute pottery shop and casino
three 6's still pay 30-to-1
just like any three of a kind.

Feeling lucky? You are
if you don't live in Shiprock.
From there it's ninety-three miles of Navajo land
and its remnants of people:
past mesas and rock-monument valleys,
sta-gro minimarts, free aerobics
and bingo at the community center,
sheep marching like muddleheads to pasture,
low-watt AM stations blaring
about flea markets and the Naschitti rodeo.

Revelation's unlucky thirteenth
does not mention the Devil,
but a man with understanding
can calculate the number of the beast,
although it is way too late to look for signs;
they've all been stolen,
and Satan's byway, once a tributary
of the Mother Road, is gone,
gone the way of thirteenth floors
and communists and Flip Wilson's Geraldine.
Who knows what the Devil made her do?
It will no longer spawn an accident or a Joad.

Still, you can miss a turn with tequila
as easily as you can with Jesus.

A spooked man fears his common-law wife
will drive off the road, defy fate (seatbelt unbuckled),
and flip into the canyon. He talks to a priest
who speaks to a legislator in confession.
The governor petitions the government.
and one hundred ninety-one miles of road,
the gradual highway to H-E-Doublehockeysticks,
gets repaved with good intentions.

It is just one of the ways things change: South Korea
adds seven soldiers so its troops in Iraq number 673,
a bus route in Moscow becomes 616, a family in Orange County
disowns its child whose Social Security number begins in sixes,
the NBA opens a store at you-guessed-where on Fifth Avenue.
Everyone suspects demons in the biochip, creatures in the bar code.

See for yourself: *W* is the twenty-third letter.
Two and three is five. Three *W*'s are fifteen.
Add the one and five, and you get 6, first sign of the fiend.
The World Wide Web, www, 666.

In South America a butterfly flaps its wings
and prays to have nothing to do with us.

If You're Drinking To Forget, Please Pay in Advance

Priests in plain clothes, insomniacs afraid to close their eyes,
refugees from the sleep club with vacant stools on either side,
parolees, defrocked veterans, women wearing little more than a nightie,
encrusted vomit in a bathroom even a MerryMaid couldn't keep tidy,
thermoses of hot coffee, beer nuts, and happy hour pizzas,
rascals on the run whispering endearments to señoritas,
first timers drinking with bikers at the bar, soldiers home on leave,
forlorn housewives escaping the kitchen table and looking for a place to grieve
where the barmaid goes to the well for another vodka and schnapps,
licks her sticky lips and primes the tip jar, putting two fives on top,
smiles at out-of-towners, blowhards, eavesdroppers making dirty calls
beneath Christmas decorations months out of season, the sounds of losers
    racking balls
and all their idle threats, swearing next time to really kick the ass
of the guardian angel on the shoulder of the smirking guy refilling his glass.

Something Charming

She said I should
    do something charming
        like fall from a pleasure boat

and flail in the wrack and reeds
    humiliating my flesh
        (where my demise

has always been portended)
    until scooped up again
        I am warmed and welcomed

by cheery onlookers
    in dry clothes
        snapping pictures.

I think of the birdbath
    where so many bees drown
        every summer,

the public fountain
    full of coins
        where death also pretends

to close its eyes.
    She wanted me to succumb
        to the slow pull of the sun

and emerge reborn, not as the man I was
    but like bearded Neptune rising,
        the wide, wide ocean all around.

Out Here

Bo Diddley walked 49 miles of barbed wire,
but out here that wouldn't get you to the next town
or even to the next ranch, and, hell,
if you got there, you'd wish you hadn't,
West Texas no place to be caught afoot.

Out here you can see beyond the horizon,
but who wants to? At Cash-and-Carry Tires
Rodney, skinny as an apple spider, beats his tire tool
on an ungaraged stack of retreads as you pass.
The slapdash ovals might get you just out of sight
but not much farther, their belts of nylon, steel, and carbon
with no more grip than three Jack-and-Cokes at the bar.

LaLa's Mexican brags it has the best food for miles,
and who could argue? But do you really want to find out?
Heat from the roadbed and the stench
of a flattened dog make the letters swim.
A kicked hubcap falls face down, warns not to take the risk.

In fact all the signs remind that you're on your own.
The lone church's message board
asks where you would go if you died.
You know the answer, but what you really want to know
is where you'd go if you coughed up blood?

You swallow hard, choking back vagrant thoughts.
Divine justice isn't the hardest part,
even though you've heard what it intends to do.
A small cloud, like an old Polaroid snapshot,
curls upon itself and darkens overhead.
You don't want to know what might develop.

You don't want to be caught out here — dead or alive —
in a town like this where no one cares where you are.
Out here the out here follows you; you can even hear it
at your heels, its stride quick and insistent.
When it reaches you is anybody's guess,
another mathematical theorem as unresolvable
as who you love, when you became a man,
and where you will spend the uncertain night.

Moonlight and Peaches

footloose as confetti
the moon falls here
the same as it does at home

do not worry, sweet babe,
God won't cry
when it does

though his tear
would be the size
of a harbor seal

and likely flood
any seafront wharf
if he did

besides it's time
we got wise to his trick
of pretending to watch over us

when your brother
stumbles through town
drunk as the last bee

of summer
God doesn't hang
over him

frozen in time and beaming
like a stopped watch
it's just the moon

we could talk to him
to both of them
tell them we're tired

of their sulking silence
one hand always threatening
to turn the knob and leave

but that's just what the moon does
it slips behind the clouds
above Mogollon

scattering reflections
like errant sheep
on the hillside

it's not the kind of light that will
strip paint or peel a shed like a peach
so it shouldn't have the last word

leave that to the hills
the dark hills, ready like us
to swallow whatever may ripen

Continental Drift

When our relationship came apart like Pangaea,
I was ordered out. Insinuations and imprecations —
ugly, lazy, unregenerate, dumb — followed
each bundle and box I carried to the car.

I bit my lip, tasting withheld blood
and the savor of a new country being formed.

When with the last armload she added, "I hope you die
a slow, miserable death," my silence broke
like a new coastline, one with a vast mainland
and a shimmering bay. "So now," I said, "you want me stay?"

Pity Poor Mercalli

The Richter Scale registers magnitude, the Mercalli Scale intensity.

How sad to be forgotten, to see at distance
another man's name upon the marquee
starring above the shaking epicenter. But experience
teaches that misery is local, always nearby, and the lack of fame
      the reckoning of someone else's fault:

like the electric fan threatening the television signal
as the opponents mount a final drive,
or the hijacked liner asail on an uncrowded sea,
the absent seat that warns when someone is not home,
the scream muffled by the cupped hand, the contagion
of rare disease, cars like closed confessionals
where the lost child waits
      and suicides rehearse.

Not every rumble moves the earth — or condemns it to doom.
But sometimes there's just no good way
to gauge the caliber of a small thing, like the shock
      of a gun fired in a closed room.

The Texas Country Reporter Interviews the Famous Poet

"Come in, come in," you said when the van
  pulled to the curb. "Iced tea?"
Just a cameraman and lone reporter
  a long way from Dallas.

Inside it's soft leather, a/c, pictures —
  family, friends, you in uniform
with your foot upon the hub of a jet
  gazing off toward the wild blue.

"Is this the street," one asks,
"where you were caught in the tar,
  where your brother rescued you?
How far to the ranch? Your herd?"
  he wonders, putting down his sweating glass.

So it's stories and not poems they have come for:
to see where the squirrel squeezed through the soffit
  and rampaged the attic all winter.
They want to see for themselves where heat lightning
  struck the old bull, all the made up things:
the windmill with damaged blades, sucker rods
complaining loudly in the wind, a pond where wild ducks
might float by, barbed wire stretching to the horizon,
  the trough where you baptized the dog.

There are no horses or cows,
  no mules — no ranch to confess to.
The camera stays unpacked, disappointed.
It wants ... not exactly lies but not truth either.
Imagine them you want to say,
  but these are men who cannot imagine
  something they've already seen.

And because the sky is overcast and irregular,
they can't even trace the clouds with a finger.
They are pointless, the sky seems to say —
so you don't have to — as you envisage
the door of an unreal barn closing.

Listen to the Trees

Listen to the trees she says,
how they whisper, their arms
enfolding one another in a canopy
of sky-supporting dreams,

two lives fashioned into one,
lovers twining on the grass below.
Listen to the trees. Listen.

I hear only their bark, she complains,
but she misunderstands. I know women
who leave like silken stems,
and poor Ariel pined for Sycorax
yet was stilled by her bewitching oath.

Your words are adzes.
They shape the indurate heart
until the whole forest gossips
and innuendoes race to every branch office.

Listen, listen to the trees. she says.
Why? I say, when trees,
trees are such liars.

Chemo Ward at Texas Children's Hospital
— for Suzanne

At the computer struggling with a poem,
I imagine you examining a child
who has surrendered to the weight of her own bones.
The protocol has failed, and the oncologist will send her home
where her psalm-swallowing parents will wait for her to die.
And though you cannot understand, you curse your faith
and my lack of it, believing that no caress
bears a sufficient dose of hope.

But vodka is not served in the gingerbread house;
crows have already lighted on the roof
and weevils spoiled the grain. The starlight
is counterfeit, and a phantom poses
with his sickle beside the last wolf in the forest.

The poem I am writing will not speak itself.
It cannot save anyone or transform the world
because it is about omissions:
the unrepaired watch, a broken bike,
not a father pulling on mismatched boots to drag
a doomed child's sled through the snow.
My poem, when it comes, will be a dispatch
to cows returning home, an ode to firewood in free verse,
one that renovates our daily artifacts into a sentence
spun from grammar's broken glass.

It will not be a monument to a martyr or saint;
this poem will not contain any living person.

Bad Coffee Is Grounds for Divorce

"If we have no peace, it is because we have forgotten we belong to each other."
— Mother Teresa

Dancing backward toward the future,
wives evade excuses, sidestep
indiscretions and infidelity,
pretend to remodel the heart of matrimony
in a lively curvet while secretly
harboring homages to Sexton and Plath.

Face it: nuclear families are for electrons
and morons. A man with street cred
doesn't stand a chance. Like the spider
that makes you shriek, he is unfit
for indoor life. He burns
unevenly like a Tibetan monk.

Watch the heart of Hamlet. No matter
how well he dances, he is a greenhead,
a filchman, a lightfooted bandog, no hero.
Wedlock is an anomic pasquil; marriage,
an idol's grave adorned with plastic flowers.

A Lot in Common

I never understood
why we couldn't get along.

We had so much in common:
we both loved her and hated me.

reel life and others

"Any idiot can face a crisis; it is this day-to-day living that wears you out."

— Anton Chekhov

Reel Life

feeling small under the moon,
I cast my attention toward the far bank
as the baited line takes another measure of fall

I congratulate myself as it misses
the driftwood nearby, the leaves pushed
by current, and tip my hat to *señor otter*

who startles like a snake,
then flees the splash
the lure makes, just a pair of infidels

trying out lines at night, repeatedly
coming up short and trying to avoid collapse,
two hustlers in a narrow river shooting craps

until, sensing we are not alone, I call in my bet,
reel in hard before turtles snapping like the vaginas of whores
can swallow the night like a box of dark chocolate

Gator Eye

his eye sees
    and having seen
closes

on a time half past
    and another where paradise
lies dreaming

the seer becomes the scene
    but having eyes
also discloses

a world where hyacinths gather
    and the great blue heron stands
just off camera blinking

Rallids in Marshes

Moorhens, limpkins, curlews, coots,
sungrebes and button quail,
reedy seas filled with purple galinules.

They've come for the harvest yield:
egrets, darters, ducks, terns,
king rails, gulls flattening every field,

and crakes descending like teeming hail.
The air is full of their grallatorial snipes,
shorebirds that call in diatonic scale

until the whole damned jury adjourns,
these wetland gotwits and phalaropes
and thousands of others who disagree by turns

and argue with the greenshank's gripes.
Like yellowleg lawyers and willets,
they are insistent as dotterels, plovers in the rice.

The grain is rife with feeding stilts,
oystercatchers, thick-knees,
herons, spoonbills, and avocets;

they quarrel like ibises in thousand-dollar suits
or natant cormorants diving for fees:
moorhens, limpkins, curlews, coots.

The Missing

Exiled, forgotten even by family,
they are left without mirrors
and youth, hidden away where we
grinning act as if they're just away,
perhaps visiting or fishing,
not vanished, not gone, not gone missing.

It's not as though their broken Cessna
circled in an uncertain longitude
and went down trying to land
on a rusty barge, pump toilet
full of octane and shit,
or that a norther caught them
on the thawing ice
without their polypro turtlenecks,
polar jackets, and fleece.

No accident, we put them
where they will not stay,
the disoriented and depressed,
the retarded, repellent, refused,
everyone for whom life got bent — all the bullies,
washed-up cowards, and drunks,
the misfired suicides with ungrammatical notes,
footloose teens, bored and dangerous,
cruel, mean, and addicted to inhalants.

They come back to us from their day jobs
and the nightshift, the warehouses and boneyards,
the hospitals where they just walk away
hopped up on smokes and caffeine
thinking every day a holiday
when they have a scaling knife or gun
(and beneath the floorboard they all carry one).

And we think we hear the absent child scream,
the solitary hitchhiker, the sound
of the shovel scraping, the whack
against the head. And the bodies, the bodies,
uneasy in the rigor of the dead
and wanting to return, eyes gorged with fear
and pushed into some fishtrap,
throats cut deep and clean, stippled
and defying gravity, hands tied behind them
and coming back to the world, rising now,
rising again from the bottom against their will
like sullen catfish in unlaced shoes.

I Remember

Every day starts like the one before:
children rise like steam off oatmeal
to the rattle of dishes and the smell of lard,
cut-up onions and sifted flour in the pan,
pepper and salt. It's a breakfast no one could curse.

I remember what my father said:
when all you have is road kill, just eat around the tread.

And every day goes on about the same.
It's hard to keep a house clean. Excuse it.
The neighbors' dust comes right in;
the dancing motes disobey the light.
The cinder road makes washing worse.

I remember what my father said:
the sleep of the just is just the sleep of the dead.

Instructions Received in a Dream

Forgetting is a kind of power too,
    like satisfaction and desire
        and the stammering shadows

they make when they wake in the night.
    Yet the thought of forgetting also distresses,
        as if our tongues

might no longer give voice to the worm
    in our mouth,
        sound like a bird,

or call like the old drake
    who waddles uneasy to his pond.
        They are,

like everything we recall,
    far off,
        a beast whose pain

was made sacred by common need.
    I once knew the color of your eyes
        then my dream left me speechless.

Estrangement

Schooled in failing
I wander
days
carpet to tile
where cat food
rankles in its dish
in a house
empty
as an amputee's sleeve:
misery is its own justice.

Nights
I catch myself
between bed and boredom
cubed ice
obscuring reflection
and recognize
in tonic admiration
my unshaven ways
the stubble
of my moral veneer.

Moving
in this nebula
of misgivings
is not easy
and
of late
I see myself
irresolute as ever
a drugstore bird

rocking foolishly
between drink and dance
in alien time
some stumbling blackbird
with detergent wings.

Belling the Vampire

Forget the cats and upland buzzards you'll see after nuclear war,
the low oaths you mutter into your tankard that will not work.
He wants a mouthful of your milk-pink lemonade
and a moonlight waltz, but, if you don't want to dance
in his deep-vein jamboree, buy yourself a glove
and an aluminum bat. Oh, sure, garlic is tasty and great
for enchiladas in molé, but one clove won't be enough,
and chants and incantations work about as well.
Get yourself a tiny brass bell. Call it self-defense
and call this a letter from an unhinged friend,
but, when you hear its tinkle, it will sound like the siren
of something surprising approaching in a mach-one spurt,
astonishing and as startling as seeing a gar in the bathtub, a white guy
making change at the U-Totem, or the pope in a Hawaiian shirt.

Subject-Verb-Complement

Consider the oddity of love's grammar:
The first person gives way to a familiar second,
Conjugating in time another *he* or *she*, an *it* perhaps,
As even gender may be set aside —
The single lover made plural, two become one.
No wonder we are confused.

Whatever person I speak in,
You are my subject, and, though I object,
No copulative links me to you,
Only to another form of myself.

When I say I love you,
The compliment is resisted,
And no matter how hard I try to verb you,
I end up speaking always in a passive voice.

At the Arcade

Nam was never like this:
    every kid with two quarters
a ready ace steadying his hand

against alien intercepts
    and ninja dragons.
The occasional mercy mission
    interrupts to hop a frog through traffic,

but mainly it's about the speed
    of assassination:
video commandos bearing down on gooks,

hippos and robots
    that swarm and divide
like Mickey's broom
    before being dispatched

into fire-spiked pits below.
    They earn their way
by lighting up the world,

fingers smoking,
    snapping off Kools
at the filter
    when things get tightest.

Not so elemental
    as bopping rodents
with a mallet

or filling clowns' heads
    with water,
but it beats sliding down
    for fun

a sanded balustrade
    in quick escape,
Dad close behind

targeting your smokes,
    or catching
penny-apiece hoppers
    on Granny's farm.

You tried your life
    and didn't like it;
Nam was never like this,
    even when it was.

Finding Your Way in the Dark

Like the devil, you know
    how to leave the road
        and cross the thawing ditch,
the fence, the long field home.

You fear the weight of stars,
    but like them you want to burn,
        set your kettles rattling and steaming,
and boil your beer-soured roots to broth.

        But the candescent god between your fingers
fears the dark, hurries it to flame.
    When you strike, something inside you
        shudders like a moth, and something matchless
dares you to call it by its name.

Hollywood Metonymic

Cozy in bed, her back curls
like an acrobat's beneath the comforter
in a nocturne of warm jasmine
and bedclothes' cologne whose cost might pay
a Medicaid mother's (or tsunami victim's) toll.

She is Darwin's pride, twenty-five,
and on the chair her tiny sequined dress
retains the movements it has committed to memory,
a walk-on part in heirloom clothes, another
trophy for something that resembles acting.

It is a town full of glass-hearted starlets
who stay up late singing to the dark
about the lingering kiss, the rock drummer's caress,
casual drugs and trapeze-artist sex
until fallen and ankle wrapped in tensor

she takes to bed — two slices
of herbal sleep and endless martinis
for the pain — until the circus landscape
transforms the room into something more curious:
the way fame takes its revenge upon doom.

Indelicate

a balloon is
so too the dandelion
tossing its seeds windward

and the woman
curving with a separate life
inside her

I see your small hands
single and rooted
tethered in bliss
floating inside
your mother's once-slender stem

like an expanding star
on your way to oblivion
with a closed fist

but demanding for a moment
the brief time to be
someone's heedless son

Family Thrift

Pig drunk and full of arson
(and minute to minute unsure),
he struck a match and stared
at the welter of insignificance
that called itself goodwill.
Then he danced about with a coal oil lamp
that made him think of his grandmother
and threw it, lit, at a mattress,
a doll, a stack of books.

The store was a rich clutter;
now it's all ashes on the curb,
something calm, almost elegant:
tea sets and suitcases, cat
carriers, discarded 8-tracks
all thickened into a single mass,
deprivation turned nearly into art,
something new from many things burnt.

The police heard his monomaniac plea,
how every household has lost a heart to history,
but confessions are less interesting
to the confessor for whom only fire
can redeem the settling world.

A life rejected by joy is seldom tolerable,
and sometimes what falls through our hands
was never welcome or was just too long in coming
and sadder than heartbreak — or an unfashionable hat.

Sorry Seconds

More bad news: the secretary's out,
her two kids down with colds,
and the ex has called twice.
"Mark time, you devil," she scolds

even before the first cup
of coffee's gone
and the copier's begun
its metronomic drone.

This is how your life
will go, it intones toward lunch,
the next like the first, only smaller,
despite your best hunch

that ten dollars could
get a bottle to do
some talking. When at last
everything lies ruined —

and it will —
there will not be clinics enough
nor liquor to heal
us all. Life is rough;

that's just how it goes.
Still it beats hearing that
the neighbor's boy
has killed another cat

or your mistress's
moronic husband
is likely to make parole.
Take it like a man.

Your doctor's lies
are sweeter than nectar,
like the laugh
that wakes you whether

you're dreaming or not.
Count your minutes, fool:
life is a fast dance that ends
just when you learn what steps to do.

You have no right to believe
in a God made impressionable
by prayer any more than
you shouldn't expect trouble

from that old, pregnant stray
you once thought so nice
who found her way to you
bearing a brief reward of mice.

Reliable Sources

if truth were to recede
like fog or bad gums
and every opinion become secret

if tolerance loosened like intertidal mud

if the contradictions were not all set
like the arms of the cross
and no one went your direction

if all the diabolists and biting angels
all the emperors in embryo were quelled
by wit sharper than a garden tool

if there was a name for what you once were

would words like faith suffice
when other guidance systems fail

This Close

She is this close to killing him,
seconds away from handing him
his hat or his head,
from aiming a glass or plate,
is inches from banishing him
to some irradiated power plant
or crematorium
and singing "The Old Double Cross"
over his frangible silicating bones,
no stench, no smell of what was
amid the pieces left broken behind.

Love ruins everything. It jumps
like a creek from its unruly bed,
turns water into rock, and sweeps away
hutch, china, and all their promises
in the wash. Controlled, it dies
like lightning bugs in a jar.

She fears fire, fights it. "Baste
in your own juices, you bastard,"
she says but does not cry.
She saves water, takes its measure,
even when she already knows
her glass is only half full.

EOTWAWKI — Dec. 21, 2012

(the end of the world as we know it)

We're past the Maya whose five-thousand-year calendar collapsed
waiting for mighty Quetzalcoatl twelve centuries back.

Then it was Nostradamus who prophesied quakes and wind,
a reversal of the poles, and high floods guaranteed to do us in.

For the Babylonians it was Nibiru, the rogue star,
their Planet X whose terrestrial collision made us as we are

and caused asteroids, the moon, and Earth
(to which astronauts behind their reflective eyeshields came to work

and extracted gold from our mines).
We plugged the BP spew just in time.

Though the ice caps slowly melt,
someone long dead is nevertheless set to read the cards we've been dealt;

just call him the poet in the distance, the one standing
ready to give his own culture transcendence.

Next Time

"I still miss my ex-husband," she said.

"Next time," I said, "aim for the torso."

enlarged hearts

"A summer wind, a cotton dress. That is how I remember you best."

— Richard Shindell

The Woman Who Disliked Kissing

beneath a tree of splendid yellows
the season turns in an outdoor café
a menu of crabs and scallops
a caravel in casual heaps
informal, harvested for sentiment
and ceremony, an evening of plum flowers
on a mirrored muraled wall

but these surfaces mean nothing
no matter how much moonlight
spills onto her heart

she is just canvas, something plain
upon which the night
repeatedly misspeaks itself
its pasty telegrams rumble through her
like a freight with many cars

she stores sadness in her pulse
is disappointed by the sweetness
that descends
                        and fearful that the autumn
interruptive and breakable as the slightest oath
has always been more secure, more trusting
than her soft uncommittable kiss

Evil Twins

long ago and far away
are a fairy tale, a couple
like dog and pony –
duplicate offspring
of debauched trolls

but if all brothers are grim
then one day may marry
another and still another
until the whole year seduces
and something misbegotten
whispers like a suicide
in the daily news

the risk is needless

when a star dies
a farmer may dream a hundred suns
to make his glum garden green

and what grows grows on credit
always borrowing
against someone else's bank

if one crop fails
something curious
nonetheless grows

until a night in a hotel
and one under a bridge
become similar perils

and what flies from the window
could be pigeons
or just old love letters
breaking in every direction

Oscar Wilde Visits Walt Whitman

432 Stevens Street, Camden, New Jersey – 18 January 1882

Removing his fur-trimmed greatcoat, he passes it
to the poet's sister and sits, twenty-seven,
a splendid boy, almost squatting on the stool
near the old poet's arm. His brown felt suit
is trimmed in pink — buttonholes and collar –
and he withdraws an opium-scented cigarette
from an inside pocket, yet another new fashion
in public vanity but one that soothed
the *mal de mer* of his crossing.

The *Arizona* was one of the largest
merchant ships afloat, although two years before
it rammed an iceberg on the third day out,
but the bulkhead held, and the forehold did not fill.

Today they speak of an ancient war,
sip milk punch and elderberry wine;
in time their tongues prophesy a new age.
"We in England," the younger says,
"think there are only two — Emerson and you."
The older, his ungroomed beard reflecting
winter's light, nods, acknowledges the salute.

And then in a theatrical moment
or one from the Hebrew texts
but lacking both chorus and statuary,
the acolyte places his left hand on the old prophet's spermary
and swears a personal vow. Later that evening
old Walt perambulates down Broadway with friends;
Wilde heads to vast Niagara to go swanning,
the kiss of Whitman still warming his lips.

A Poem of Small Promise

our steps are made of fine stuff and as we walk
the town is quiet like Shangri-la after a rain
and from doorways come the aromas of steaming fish
where overdue bottleflies dance along the rims of discarded glass

cats gather in flower pots to knead the moist soil
and when we place our lips upon each other's
under this comfortable moon the streetlight on us
is like an evening's aperitif that asks *what is that taste?*

a secret — just like what lies beyond the neighborhood gate
where a paddock of llamas friendlily press the fence
for food and a brief caress

it is the scene we have both been dreaming
and when I step back I see the day we are about to live,
a Georgia girl and a giant peacock preening

Death-Defying

The optimist believes we live in the best of all possible worlds;
the pessimist fears this is true.

The Nazis, clever boys, tried
to revive dying soldiers by covering
them with naked Jewesses whose
young bodies – if anything – might raise the dead.
It is an experiment that likely left both sides confused
and led to calling death a rhetorical predicament,
a linguistic displacement by which Paul deMan could excuse
his anti-Semitism as deconstruction of the Jews:
just another example of how the extraordinary rarely
defines the quality of life or the tightness of the noose.

No one wants to die on the first of the month.
Many old bags look alike. Happiness hides
like red meat at Lent. Bigamy is merely one husband
too many. And no amusement seems quite as astonishing
as the idea of Irene and her copulating donkeys.
(Another day, another daughter.)

The slacker's *Rubaiyat* promises bread
and wine, not water, and jugs of it (*wow!*)
and you loafing beside in near undress — *paradise and how*!

So if the water is warm, maybe it's because
hell is just below. But keep in mind
that brain damage is less likely in a cold bed.
Still onward we go, all playing our parts,

though in truth, our great loves won't kill us young;
we'll go slowly, sovereign as oranges
but cracking inside all along like pyramids
or undeliverable valentines with enlarged hearts.

No One Else To Say It

Because there is no one else to say it,
my barber tells me
that love will wreck our lives.

Never give more
than they can use he says,
and he might know:
thickset like a wrestler
and muscular as a starfish,
he looks strong enough
to ride muleback over the Andes.

He is without hair himself,
skin the color of a wild carrot,
but I am in the pulpit
of a man who's had
his heart cut out
and survived the strike.

You wouldn't order a meal
on the recommendation
of a skinny waitress, would you?
In the mirror I try to follow
his muffled alphabet,
the paths his clippers take.

Then he tells me again
how he's beaten the odds,
love and heart disease.
So I listen when he says to bet
heavy on Big Roger in the fifth.

Running with Scissors

After bath when I hold you from behind
and fix you in this afternoon's caress,
our pleasure has no need or hurry. Your
skin, hot and radiant, bends to entice,
and the light leans into something so sure
in the angles of your elbows and legs
that, when I assemble us in our love,
I believe one woman at last enough,
this slowness unavoidable and blind
like our bodies folding into
each other's arms without risk.

Close now, we could not pare ourselves apart
even if we knew the hazards that lie
in this illusion we have made. Happy
and distrustful of being loved alone,
we linger in its long allure.

But watch, heart, what sudden perils arrive
when disaster pulses in a pinched vein.
The closer I hold you and more secure,
the clearer I also see tragedy's bloody face.
The air comes quick, and something truly sharp
threatens should I fall. It is a strange race —
to you and then away — shaky with danger,
as both of us circle the whetted edge of pain.

Letter to B.

All I need is freedom and fresh eggs,
Fertile things that make the world taste clean
And fragile like the blush in my heart.

When the wind lifts the trees here,
It says how long and easy love is,
Also how very hard; the short ones stand it best.
Tonight I bend in memory toward the dark

Where, rooted at distance, I sway toward home
Hoping that what blows through me today
Will reach your arms in time

And asking in the leaves winding back
To you a small indulgence, a chance,
Another waltz at the window,
One more dance.

Unmade Love

Coming together
in its name they
kissed, swore,
and declared it
made.

Then somehow the elixir soured,
the residence
divided by a writ.
The attorneys disputed
what every sentiment
originally had meant.

What law
has joined,
man eventually puts aside,
and once denied
love proves a small coin

too scant to close
the deal.
It comes; it goes.
They signed
upon the line
but could not forget the feel

of twelve years of bad road.
Marriage is sad, they say,
and leaving is a busy street.
Its wayfarers are the wrong turns
you meet while hauling someone else's load.

Vuelta

1. Spring Again

sometimes it's good to turn away
from things about to disappear
darkness always comes late
and from great distance

but the romantic says
sweet the night but cruel the day
because he's seen sunlight
poach the lilies on his mother's grave

light is dependable that way
can be counted on to signal
when trouble is nearby

but it also deceives
encourages us to play dress up
to see ourselves as angels

ascending into the idea
of how we might live —
which is the very hardest thing to bear

2. Idle Time

nothing ever happens here

on the orphan branch
of this family tree
no one to clean up after

even at the ice house the girls
hardly ever talk to you
though you hear them laugh
about inner tubes and sandals

you imagine thongs, roundness
emerging from bikini tops

but fun is a package deal
and eventually even
comes to bore

and when the beer begins
to reason with your dreams

you know that despite your best denial
you just cannot run off a homeless cat

3. Planetary Texas

there it is – the order of the universe intact
the farthest planet reaching forward
the surf clambering up the receding beach

onshore hanging onions flake their psoriatic skin
teenagers blush like the cheeks of tangerines
patterned granite swirls pink, sometimes gray
and melons open wide perfecting original sin

no one seems to care if this is heaven

4. A Bad Business Model

the plan's a little sketchy:

curse the passing cars
practice his smoker's cough
and trace decades of decay
in the mirror's line   wash seldom
and only in darkness
collect state capital plates
and Grand Prize cans
(rarer than rocking-horse excrement)
wait for the lost girls
to find their way home

a man should never buy or sell insurance
if there are no prospects of conversion

5. A Note To Say

I'm sorry not to have written sooner

shame and obscurity
keep me pretty busy

at twenty-two
we honeymooned in Hawaii
and drank from coconuts on the lanai
watched the ocean
recede into the undisturbed horizon

a life that compelled rejection followed

today Gulf minnows
swarm the shallows
nibbling at what they hope
may be in my hand

I write of course to see
how you're doing
and to whisper
what I didn't say long ago

6. A New Cosmology

we're following the progress
of a little bolt of orange above the shore
maybe a frosted balloon
or someone's pet bird —
perhaps the discolored bruise of a canary
or some sort of stain

it could be
the last thread of the sun
mending something about to lose color
where light and cloud
fold into one another in midair
and trail translucent wings

the dog barks twice
as if sensing the earth's shift

7. Alternatives to Anticipation

change could happen any day
the invitation come at any time
now that you are far too old to care

what matters
is that her lips once parted
without embarrassment

and when she kissed you
you knew the joy
of the right word's arrival

and later the shame
that follows
every wasted night

8. Honk if You Love Satan

I know well this old ballet,
this dance of serpents:

the crosshairs of the inexorable meter
clicking as we taxi across
shattered gutterglass glistening
on skin-shedding sheets of rain

while the traffic snakes and coils
in afternoon flood
up the avenue
catching red lights all the way

I'd flay them all
into a good hatband

9. Winter Again

is it light or love
that gets us
through another season

the room opens to both
and sweet breezes stir the drapes
in the place where the hired woman

once spoke her confessions
full of false eyelashes and betrayal
indignation trembling on her skin

and someone else wanting to be kissed
we were three characters in the tale
of a single human ache

The Problem of Angels

Her reflection in a porcelain bowl
a figurine-like face
with hair of pearly china strands
and polished wisps finely placed.
Like a faceted mirror she reflects
crystalline images in inexpensive glass.
And yet we stoop with careful hand
to hold protectively in deep-cupped palms
cherished gifts we cannot understand,
discarded whims of little matter
and fear to touch them else they shatter.

In the All Seasons Motel

They are sad, the stories of my friends,
and largely true, their lives
diaries read in soft dismay.

Waking in rooms of small pleasure,
they mean to collect what is owed,
what was sworn to they cannot forego.

And they have, I think, a right to some joy,
to whatever launders
their hard memories of youth and home.

They are sad, the stories of my friends,
and sometimes true; they lie like lies
in diaries from lips redder than softest May.

At the End

Joining the old just before the end,
you arrive with your belly full of blood,
wonder why no one was standing guard.
There was scarcely even time to pack

or occasion to say how hard
it was to keep safe to the very end.
No one dies as he deserves, though
some in fact go without marks at all,

but you, you fear, came all too lightly,
lacked a plan to set yourself apart.
It is too late now to talk of
schemes that separated like the races

or what you wish you had been stowed in your heart.
You saved something you thought was love,
but what remained was little, just this —
a dream endeared by warm embraces,
a woman you never met blows a kiss.

What We Said

we both said things
neither of us meant

I said I can't live without you
she said prove it

absorbed, inhaled, or ingested

"What we call a way is only a hesitation."

— Franz Kafka

Monoxide

you ride
into our suburbs
on grills
ovens and chainsaws

burn with a flare
so yellow
we hardly notice

tasteless
and colorless
as a Republican

you promise warmth
but deceive

no odor or stench
a mere popcorn fart
of a flame

until absorbed
inhaled or ingested
our mouth forms
your single exhausted O

and we lie down before you
with heavy, heavy eyes
and fluttering heart

Crossing Frozen Water

Fallen again, legs open like scissors, I gather myself
and rise, try to catch up, and call across the frozen glaze.
My leather soles skip, unbalanced on the slippery waves,
as I inch from foot to foot. Once a river, the ice
threatens to tump me yet again, stares like an ancient god.

If this temporary sidewalk gets me to the other side and you,
I promise I'll pay him back. But facts blur with fiction.
The darkness below the freeze seems to have a human face;
it bares its teeth and smiles as down again I go.

I return my body to its rightful owner, reassemble, and adjust
my cap, utter another curse, voice quavering in the chill.
I vow to break the water's bones, but I'm always tougher
close to shore. I'll pay him back. I swear to God I will.

My Grandmother's Song

my grandmother got up early
and sang to the well pump's crank
the water sang too

the clothes she washed
came clean and hung
joyfully on the slack line

but when she snared an old hen's ankle
with a wire hook
the soup tasted like rooster wash

happiness for her
was nothing more than
a speck of something

just beginning to appear
down the road
something no larger

than the sun's promise
sealed like a parcel
or the prospect of a package

beneath whose lid
the new day sang
like a chorus of baby chicks

Bad Day at the Psychic Fair

In the saucer where Madame Rhoda reads
the leaves, glum onlookers gather and tend
to the unfolding future of a friend.
"The crowd is larger than I expected.
We didn't foresee so many," I catch
her say. I wince, the gaffe undetected
by the spiritualist in black beads
or Sister Geneva tapping her watch.

At two tables tattling women roll dice,
men in mascara cut cards left to right;
one fellow reads irises by flashlight,
offers to do a woman and her dog.
Others balance chakras across the room
by means of an unseen ionic fog
telepathically bargaining price.
Incense surrounds like the dark dusk of doom.

Rama the Realtor is a specialist.
Guided by a spirit that cannot spell,
he consults his bad ouija to foretell
property deals, doesn't know *lien* from *lean*.
Though his fingers skate across each letter,
he flounders to decipher what they mean,
sighs like a girl, says s's with a lisp,
winks at the man in the cashmere sweater.

I choose the Latina with the plain face.
Her earrings snag the candlelight like hope;
I see she has sized me up for the dope
I likely am. She points with a low laugh

to the skull tattoo on her exposed breast
and sips a cordial from a small carafe.
She leans forward. "Let's start with an embrace,"
she says and thrusts herself into my chest.

When she drags her sharp nail across my life,
my love-lines race toward certain disaster
as if she knows what I mean to ask her.
She sees colliding stars within my house
and notes the empty ringfinger's divorce.
I keep staring into her drooping blouse
while she calculates yet another wife,
the cost to put my heart before the whores.

I think I know what I want her to say:
there'll be happiness, maybe even love
(or surrogate passions that also move),
at least the timely promise of a raise.
She says that she can set my future free.
And when she puts my hand to her broad waist,
I know what it is she will do for pay.
My future never stood so firm to see.

But mystery still baffles all the while —
what she says is just what she sees, no more.
And I listen as if I want still more —
more of me, of the world, more of something
this woman claims to know, as if she could
say anything that wasn't demeaning
and not suppose her dress was out of style
while hope collapses — as we knew it would.

Another Thing To Lament

we come to familiar spots to remember
where apprentice angels once gathered
like mosquitoes after a rain
believing the water would never stop

an old house, its slats like hachures
marks some kind of spot
where we could daily dream
the reappearance of ourselves

or see God as something more
than an Oklahoma senator
a perpetual underachiever
who wants us to change

but has run short of commandments
unlike time whose soft petitions
like the water of this deluge
never stanched any flood

Natural Selection

I sound like more fun than she does she chirps
leaving me puzzled how fun might sound

then suddenly the sky fills with flying things
iridescent bugs and birds of all color
vaulting in restless chase

they chitter and call like the buzz
of the crowd when the wirewalker
looks like he might fall but regains balance

and for a moment hangs in the air
like the last note of a cantata
before everything swarms and dives again and again

and gasps with a glee that will not stop
all that swallowing and song
the swell of hungering senses

until the great undoing arrives
and I answer her
with a question of my own

what is the lifespan of a bug?
knowing well that it depends
on just how much of a pest it proves to be

Walking the Dead Rails

imagine the first man
at the other end
of these parallel lines
where the horizon
releases everything
and time loses speed

from this spot
the loading dock sinks
locomotiveless as a drunk
under a sun laden with secrets
and the mill spur
glints in ambient light

the day smells of grass
weary with seed

the enemies of flower
are a sad generation
they hang like old fences
all post and rust
in a catchpenny past

so why should the dead feel cheated
when nature's retrieval system
is full of things that do not last

no matter where you stand
every point is a terminus
even along these dozing rails
where patches of purple
burgeon into memory
and a caudex of perennials clambers
like a cow onto the corroding trestle

it doesn't take long to go far
though it may take forever to start
everything means to thrive
until its last day
when it rises above itself
and splits the world
just like Adam's plow

Misery, Putting Oneself Out Of

Amazed by the familiar, we never expected
to see you bordered by chalk,
unpenitent as ever, on the sidewalk

flanked now by two policemen. Then one balks,
walks backward, swallows an imprecation,
a bare murmur or sussuration

of another word for fornication
as he goes. You found life
more inconvenient than an aging wife

but couldn't choose the wristline knife
or gun when a high window's
open frame, cop-strung yellow

tape flitting below,
would do. The eye sees little difference,
draws no nuance or inference

between what you meant
and how you now coldly lie, a divide
that spans what you meant to hide

and what we all can see. Facts collide
on this hard path that became your crude
way out, and what you once rued

may now no longer be overlooked or misconstrued.
Plain truth often falls flat, unresurrected;
we are amazed by the familiar we never expected.

Andrea del Sarto Lectures about Poetry

Taking roll the first day, he sees the plunge of her blouse
and underlines her name twice as he goes. Fifty-one,
he is reminded by the morning mirror's dirty joke,
the bald spot he cannot see, the paunch he won't.
Though today's lesson is Victorian, its irony is not lost,
not utterly. In love is where he thinks he wants to be.

For today he is Andrea, his lecture less a recitation
than a plea to all the Lucrezias before him,
so sibilant and dangerous, but to be their lover
is all he craves to be. He stole from a king
to woo a faithless trull who bore all the charms of vulgarity
(or worse) — desiring to paint something out of love
before her tendrils could curl around him like a curse.

He wanted a mere thing, a kindness so rare
as to go unsurpassed, and, when he says aloud,
"Don't we all?" a laugh breaks from the class,
crosses her dimpling cheeks, and moves
along the rougey line between eye and ear that
only those facing her can see.

But what can an artist or teacher do — since no one means
to learn from a verse — to keep liars from sinning
against themselves? And what's a poem for
if not to speak of love first? Ecstasy might be possible
if they lay in the dirt awhile — an afternoon say —
yet when he tries to imagine God, he sees both Him and her,
one always just a little too close and ready
to blemish his worship by returning his gaze.

Writer's Block

past midnight
into a rainy Tuesday

he stares at the page
distressed by the lack of sound
unable to rouse
his mind with a word

others have garrets
against which the talling trees
scratch their relief

some have cats that cry
like muses of inspiration
and spread themselves
like stains on tabletops

or demanding clocks
to waken them
from drowsy mistresses
to work

but this seems as real
as the nothing God faced

and what did he do
before the first creation
before the poem hit the door
swearing out of its skull

before midnight
passed into Monday
and he thought of rain

About the Author

Jerry Bradley is Professor of English at Lamar University. He is the author of six books including *The Movement: British Poets of the 1950s* and his acclaimed volumes of poetry: *Simple Versions of Disaster* and *The Importance of Elsewhere*. He is a member of the Texas Institute of Letters and past president of the Texas Association of Creative Writing Teachers. He has been poetry editor of *Concho River Review* since 1999 and was founder and editor for sixteen years of *New Mexico Humanities Review*. Bradley has served as a member of the literature panel for the Texas Commission on the Arts and the New Mexico Arts Division and is past president of the Conference of College Teachers of English and the Southwest Popular Culture Association.

Among many awards Jerry Bradley has received during his distinguished career are the CCTE Frances Hernandez Teacher-Scholar of the Year (2005), the Texas College English Association Joe D. Thomas Scholar-Teacher of the Year (2000), the Boswell Poetry Prize (1996), and the CCTE British Literature Award (1996). He has been nominated for numerous Pushcart Prizes and was named Outstanding Alumnus of Midwestern State University's College of Liberal Arts (2002).

Bradley's poetry has appeared in many literary magazines including *New England Review, American Literary Review, Modern Poetry Studies, Poetry Magazine*, and *Southern Humanities Review*.

jerry.bradley@hotmail.com
www.jerrybradley.net

The Importance of Elsewhere

Bradley's form expressively fits its subject ... striking images and sounds ... interwoven rhymes that are worthy of John Keats ... All of these works illuminate Frost's notion of metaphor, of saying one thing in terms of another. Bradley's handling of figurative language, then, enables him simultaneously to express deep emotion and to do so artfully, not sentimentally.

    Matthew Brennan, *American Poetry Review*

In *The Importance of Elsewhere* Bradley maintains an exemplary standard of literary excellence. His diction is muscular and lean, artfully absent even the slightest hint of carelessness. Whether working in free verse or executing the rigorous demands of the sonnet or rhymed triplet, Bradley writes with the consummate poetic skill of a master.

    Larry D. Thomas, Texas Poet Laureate 2008

... daring but mature talent that new poets could study with benefit and seasoned poets will undoubtedly admire ... Bradley refuses to dodge the hard questions, to make them other than they are ... his strong gift for metaphor ... Jerry Bradley is one of our state treasures.

    Jan Seale, *Texas Books in Review*

Bradley is an exceptionally fine poet whose major fault as a poet is that he waits too long between books ... beautifully written and poignant ... Bradley's poetry twists and turns on a sharp pinprick of wit that lifts it from the everyday personal poetry we have become accustomed to ... filled with moments of grace ... a book that rewards many readings for its wit, its compassion, its basic honesty, but mostly because of the poet's firm control of language and the basic, down to earth, rightness of the poems.

    Palmer Hall, *Yanaguana Literary Review*

Bradley moves seamlessly between nostalgia, humor, hope, and sorrow ... the beauty and pain of daily life ... he pushes us to see simple truths.

    John Wegner, *Concho River Review*

Highly recommended for poetry lovers and libraries.

    Janet Turk, *Review of Texas Books*

Simple Versions of Disaster

... powerful and haunting poems.
Books of the Southwest

Bradley's poetry implies that artistic creation is redemptive for the artist, including the poet, and an inspiration for us all.
Betsy Colquitt, *Texas Books in Review*

Jerry Bradley's poems seem to give up their message readily to the reader, but then they keep ringing with the grace of their style and the ripples of their meanings. I think Bradley should be recognized as one of the charter members of the New Clarity School of Poetry.
Richard Sale, *University of North Texas Press*

What is contained in this delightful collection of poetic observations is ... a remarkable wisdom that emerges from experiencing the disasters of everyday life.
Clay Reynolds, *Fort Worth Star-Telegram*

... a volume of poetry that hits the eye with a fresh view of life that even a poetry hater can love ... This book is a fine example of what purpose contemporary poetry must have, a relevancy to modern life.
Texas Writer's Newsletter

I like the wit, toughness, sensitivity, and complexity.
Dick Heaberlin, *Western American Literature*

... an interesting range of formal strategies, from open-form stanzas to cinquains and sonnets.
R. S. Gwynn, *Review of Texas Books*

How breathlessly this poet speaks. ... Lines of uncommon pungency jump out at the reader, forcing the reader to re-read their contexts. ... This is mighty fine writing.
David Castleman, *Dusty Dog Reviews*

Poetry from Lamar University Press

Alan Berecka, *With Our Baggage*

David Bowles, *Flower, Song, Dance: Aztec and Mayan Poetry* (a new translation)

Jeffrey DeLotto, *Voices Writ in Sand*

Mimi Ferebee, *Wildfires and Atmospheric Memories*

Ken Hada, *Margaritas and Redfish*

Michelle Hartman, *Disenchanted and Disgruntled*

Janet McCann, *The Crone at the Casino*

Erin Murphy, *Ancilla*

Dave Oliphant, *The Pilgrimage, Selected Poems: 1962 – 2012*

Carol Reposa, *Underground Musicians*

Jan Seale, *The Parkinson Poems*

For information on these and other Lamar Press books go to www.LamarUniversityPress.Org

Other Books by Jerry Bradley

The Importance of Elsewhere

Famous Writers of American Literature
with Samio Watanabe and Jerry Craven

Famous Writers of British Literature
with Samio Watanabe and Jerry Craven

The Movement: British Poets of the 1950s

Simple Versions of Disaster

www.ingramcontent.com/pod-product-compliance
Lightning Source LLC
Chambersburg PA
CBHW020944090426
42736CB00010B/1259